THE GREAT PACIFIC AIR OFFENSIVE OF WORLD WAR II

Volume 1

Return to the Philippines 1944

John W. Lambert

Schiffer Military History
Atglen, PA

Dustjacket artwork by Steve Ferguson, Colorado Springs, CO.

WESTY'S WAY
Depicted is the P-40 F WARHAWK flown by newly promoted Capt. Robert Westbrook in the 12 June engagement near Russel Island when he accounted for his fifth aerial victim. In the ensuing seventeen months, Westbrook's extended tours would include squadron and group commands while accruing two more kills in Warhawks and another thirteen kills in P-38 Lightnings to lead all in the 13th Air Force. Four times an ace and a now a lieutenant colonel, fate and enemy groundfire brought him down, once and for all, near Makassar Island in the Celebes, on 22 November 1944.

Acknowledgments
We are indebted to the following individuals and organizations for assistance in providing photos and information: Jim Alford, Don Anderson, Bill Balden, Mrs. J.V. Bigford, George Chandler, Jim Crow, Bill Hess, James Kendall, Jim Lansdale, Joe Maita, Ernie McDowell, Henry Sakaida, Lew Sanders, Ken Sanford, Felix Scott, Dr. Norman Sterrie, Barrett Tillman, U.S. National Archives (NARS), Washington, DC; the Museum of Naval Aviation (MNA), Pensacola, Florida; Air Force Museum, Wright-Patterson, Ohio,U.S. Air Force (USAF); U.S. Navy (USN); and the U.S. Marine Corps (USMC).

Book design by John W. Lambert.
Cover design by Robert Biondi.

Copyright © 2005 by John W. Lambert.
Library of Congress Catalog Number: 2005924764.

Printed in China.
ISBN: 0-7643-2266-4

We are always looking for people to write books on new and related subjects. If you have an idea for a book, please contact us at the address below.

Published by Schiffer Publishing Ltd.
4880 Lower Valley Road
Atglen, PA 19310
Phone: (610) 593-1777
FAX: (610) 593-2002
E-mail: Info@schifferbooks.com.
Visit our web site at: www.schifferbooks.com
Please write for a free catalog.
This book may be purchased from the publisher.
Please include $3.95 postage.
Try your bookstore first.

In Europe, Schiffer books are distributed by:
Bushwood Books
6 Marksbury Ave.
Kew Gardens
Surrey TW9 4JF
England
Phone: 44 (0)20 8392-8585
FAX: 44 (0)20 8392-9876
E-mail: Bushwd@aol.com.
Free postage in the UK. Europe: air mail at cost.
Try your bookstore first.

FOREWORD

World War II in the Pacific began with an attack by Japanese aircraft carrier units against Oahu on7 December 1941. From that time until the conclusion of hostilities in August 1945 the conflict was dominated by air power strategy for both the Allies and the Japanese. In the final analysis Allied air power proved decisive in achieving victory

There were no land masses in the broad reaches of the Pacific Ocean where great armies could clash, unlike the struggles in North Africa, Eastern Europe or the Western Front. The battles in the adjacent China-Burma-India theater of operations were the sole exception.

By mid 1942 the post Pearl Harbor Japanese juggernaut had reached to Australia and Southeast Asia. The Allies finally held the line, during the aircraft carrier conflicts in the Coral Sea and at Midway and with desperate ground actions in New Guinea and the Solomons Islands, and by 1943 the Japanese were forced on the defensive.

This volume depicts the Allied offensive drive that followed. In this vast region there were no islands where more than a handful of infantry divisions would meet in face-to-face struggles, New Guinea, the Philippines, and Okinawa being the most notable exceptions. In these and other islands ground forces engaged in bitter fighting in appalling terrain under dreadful conditions. But the strategic plan of General Douglas MacArthur and Admiral Chester Nimitz was not to seize territory but airfields or ground that would lend itself to the construction of airfields. They were viewed as the strategic stepping stones to Japan. Aviation engineers often worked under fire to hew new air bases out of jungle, coral, or volcanic rock. With each new airfield complex the range of Allied land-based aircraft was advanced,

permitting new areas of Japanese territory to come under air attack.

Even the titanic naval battles of the Pacific were primarily contests between carrier-based forces. Only in a handful of encounters did large fleets of warships engage each other in brief surface gun battles.

In virtually every Pacific campaign, the Allied air forces sought to achieve aerial supremacy, interdict Japanese maritime supply lines, and isolate the battlefield. When this was accomplished enemy ground forces were either destroyed by air power or bypassed. Some Japanese-held islands were never invaded and their garrisons never engaged. They could neither attack nor retreat because of the supremacy of Allied air power Thus they were left to wither in the wake of the advance. With hindsight it became apparent that Allied air power had become so dominant that some islands were invaded needlessly.

The targets of both carrier-based and land-based Allied air forces were largely tactical until the island-hopping strategy allowed B-29 Superforts to begin the final strategic aerial campaign against Japanese home island-industry in late 1944.

Along the path of the Pacific Allied advance air battles never achieved numbers approaching the thousand-plane strategic air raids that were launched from England. Still the air campaigns for domination of the Solomons and New Guinea were fought until the virtual destruction of one air force or the other. Likewise carrier vs. carrier battles generally saw the near annihilation of the losers air groups.

By late 1942 both Japanese and U.S. Navy aircraft carrier units had been dramatically reduced by the early contests: Coral Sea, Midway, Santa Cruz. The Japanese, however, had few carrier replacements while United States shipbuilding capacity began to spawn dozens of new carriers that would scourge the central Pacific with near impunity.

In 1943 the Allies seized the initiative from the Japanese in the Southwest Pacific with victories in New Guinea and the Solomons and began the offensive drive that would breach Japan's Pacific defense ring in the Carolines.

Subsequent carrier battles, such as the First Battle of the Philippine Sea, found hundreds of aircraft engaged on both sides. The Allied approach to the Philippines was a magnet for Japanese reserve squadrons from Formosa, China and the home islands. It was here that the desperate Japanese began to employ Kamikaze tactics.

By the end of 1944 Allied air power had advanced the bomb line to the Japanese homeland, with new carrier task forces, a continuous string of new island air bases, and new and improved aircraft. Once the air offensive reached Japan hundreds of aircraft clashed in the skies over Kyushu and Honshu.

This is a pictorial history of those intrepid airmen and the aircraft that battled for control of the Pacific Ocean during the great Allied air offensive of World War II..

These photos have been obtained from the private collections of veterans and from various official archives, all noted in "Acknowledgments." Some archival views may have been previously published, since they are in the public domain. Information accompanying official photos was frequently cryptic, incomplete, or incorrect. However, extensive research has provided historically accurate captions unseen in other works.

The reader should keep in mind that these photos, whether taken by professionals with superior cameras or by veterans as amateur snapshots, were all created under less than favorable conditions and have suffered first the ravages of the tropics and then the passage of half a century. Action pictures in particular often have obvious flaws in quality. They can not be staged. Some combat photos were made with hand held cameras, but many were taken by fixed cameras mounted in the tail, wing, or nose of various aircraft. The range of fixed cameras was estimated and set prior to takeoff. Once airborne, the camera was activated by the pilot, but he could not adjust for focus nor worry about positioning the target down sun.

Regardless of any imperfections, these rare photos provide a unique visual record of World War II in the Pacific, a conflict wherein air power proved to be the decisive factor.

CONTENTS

CHAPTER 1

FINALE IN NEW GUINEA AND THE SOLOMONS

The defeat of large Japanese ground forces in New Guinea and the Solomon Islands by lesser numbers of Allied troops was possible because the Allies controlled the air and eventually the sea lanes. Repeated Japanese attempts at reinforcement and resupply had been thwarted by aerial battering of Japanese logistical bases, like Rabaul, and the relentless hunt for enemy shipping by air units of all services.

As the Japanese gave ground grudgingly, the Allies made a series of end runs in both New Guinea and the Solomons to invest themselves beyond major concentrations of ground forces and isolate a starving enemy. Landings at Hollandia and Biak on the Northern Coast of New Guinea and at Bougainville and the Green Islands, and finally New Britain and New Ireland, served to advance the string of new air bases. These strategic moves surrounded and doomed Japanese troops in numerous pockets.

The 5th and 13th Air Forces and Marine shore-based units were expanding from the pitiful few squadrons of the early days. By early 1944, the AAF alone had seven fighter groups and twelve bombardment groups in the Southwest Pacific.

As the numbers of aircraft and crews swelled, the quality of equipment arriving from the U.S. also improved. Trial and error weapons systems had been tested in the field on bombers and then applied to modifications at the Hawaiian or Townsville, Australia air depots. By 1944 the improvements were being factory installed in new model North American B-25s and Douglas A-20s and Consolidated B-24s. Fighter aircraft that were outperformed by the Mitsubishi Zero (the P-400, P-39, P-40, Buffalo, and Wildcat) were replaced with new models that were superior to enemy aircraft in all respects — P-38s, P-47s, P-61s, Corsairs, and Hellcats.

By the end of 1944, Allied air power had won air supremacy in the Southwest Pacific. The once powerful Japanese air forces of New Guinea and the Solomons had been annihilated, committing their remaining isolated army garrisons to starvation.

Above: To further isolate Rabaul, and clear the water route along the Northern coast of New Guinea, the Allies invaded Cape Gloucester on the Western tip of New Britain. B-25s of the 38th Bomb Group cover the landing force at Cape Gloucester, New Britain in late December 1943. (NARS)
Below: By early 1944, Japanese air strength in New Guinea was seriously reduced, the loss of experienced air crews being the major cause. A damaged Nakajima Ki-43 Oscar of the 77th Fighter Sentai lies abandoned at a New Guinea airfield. (NARS)

Left: The scourge of the Solomons-Bismarcks, VF-17 was the Navy's highest scoring fighter squadron. Its first deployment from October 1943 to March 1944 was with Vought F4U Corsairs under Lt. Cdr. Tom Blackburn. It operated from bases on New Georgia and Bougainville, claiming 152 victories. Number 29 is Lt. (jg) Ira Kepford's Corsair. A 1945 sea-going tour in Hellcats netted 161 more kills for VF-17. (NARS)

A line of 35th Squadron, 8th Fighter Group. P-40Ns at Cape Gloucester, New Britain Is. early in 1944. Note the PSP used to create a landing ground at a very muddy base. (Bill Hess)

The last fighter group to be assigned to the AAF in the SWP was the 58th, arriving late in 1943. It was given a tactical support role.
Above: An early P-47D-2-RE of the 69th Squadron wore a dark olive drab paint job. (Warren Bodie via AFM)
Below: Later in the campaign the OD has weathered on a 310th Squadron P-47D-21-RA, PIED PIPER. (Ernie McDowell)

9

Above: Two new Douglas A-20 units enhanced the ranks of the 5th AF, the 312th Bomb Group (one of its aircraft seen above) late in 1943 and the 417th Bomb Group early in 1944. Gen. Kenny had made know his preference for the strafers and they arrived ready to fight. These G models were coming from the factory with six fixed forward-firing .50 caliber guns and a pair of .50s in a rear Martin power turret. (Bill Hess)
Below: The 312th Bomb Group soon adorned its aircraft with a skull and crossbones designed around the nose armament. (NARS)

The 5th Air Force's veteran 90th Bomb Group got new replacement model Liberators as the campaign for New Guinea progressed west. Above: A B-24D, SN 41-23849, with part of her final crew, (l. to. r.) officers KcKinnon, Hevenes, and Brown, completed 100 missions. (Jim Crow)
Below: PRETTY BABY, a J model, SN 42-109987 of the 319th Squadron, had racked up a respectable number of sorties by late 1944. She was the second Liberator in the 90th to bear that name. (USAF)

Left: The view of Dagua A/D, Wewak, N.G. from a 345th Bomb Group B-25 on 3 February 1944. The Ki-61 Tony fighters are from the 78th Hiko Sentai and the Nakajima Ki 49 Helen, already aflame, served with the 7th Hiko Sentai. (NARS)

A-20s of the 3rd Bomb Group raided Hollandia in March 1944 catching this row of Mitsubishi Ki-21 Sally bombers in the open. (NARS)

Above: A 3rd Bomb Group Havoc, its bomb bay doors still open, departs Hollandia over Humboldt Bay, N.G. on 3 April 1944. (NARS)
Below: A Japanese Nakajima Ki-49 Oscar engages in a very low-level dogfight with a B-25 of the 78th Squadron, 38th Bomb Group. over Hansa Bay, N.G. Both survived this encounter. (NARS)

Left: Allied air attacks on Hollandia, N.G. in April 1944 included this view of a Dinah with parafrag bombs floating from the low-level 5th AF attacker. (NARS)

Below: The Ki-46 Dinah was a handsome product of Mitsubishi, encountered on every Pacific battle front. Late versions had a max. speed approaching 400 mph. Designed for reconnaissance, it was later adapted to fight B-29s over Japan. This one was captured and repaired at Hollandia by the 3rd Bomb Group and turned into a transport for the 89th Squadron. (Author's collection)

Right: This VT-10 Avenger landed back aboard *Enterprise* despite severe damage received from a Navy Hellcat in a case of mistaken identity during Hollandia landing operations in April 1944. (Bill Balden)

On 21 May 1944 an Oscar is seen at Kamiri A/D, Noemfoor Is. just seconds before it is destroyed by parachute fragmentation bombs of a 5th Air Force A-20. (NARS)

Left: B-25 strafers of the 823rd Squadron, 38th Bomb Group pepper the superstructure of this large freighter, anchored off Sorong, New Guinea in July 1944. Crews for the several machine guns on top of the bridge appear to have been driven from their posts. (NARS)

Right: Modest attempts at camouflage were wasted on this small Japanese freighter. A bomb explodes close to the port side of the ship, and parafrags can be seen descending near the stern and in the foreground. A 13th Squadron, 3rd Bomb Group A-20 delivered the attack near Manokwari, New Guinea on 9 June 1944. (NARS)

Left: In a view over the tail, an RAAF Beaufighter races across a Japanese A/D in the Moluccas in July 1944. Ground crews sprint for cover and a Mitsubishi Ki-7 Topsy transport begins to burn. (RAAF via NARS)

The oil installations at Boela on Ceram Is., west of New Guinea, were targets for the 3rd Bomb Group on 14 July 1944. The raiders were led by CO, Lt. Col. Dick Ellis. Sweeping in low, some A-20s went for the off shore oil derricks (above) while others concentrated on oil storage tanks, pipelines, and pumping stations (below). With an escort of 475th Fighter Group Lightnings warding off Japanese interceptors, the 3rd Group did great damage and left massive fires. (Both photos from author's collection)

12A   312TH. BOMB GROUP BOELA 14 JULY

By 1944 Marine squadrons like VMSB-235 (on its fourth tour of combat) had moved up to Green Island for close range work on Japanese bases at New Britain and New Ireland. Above: It still operated the dependable Douglas SBD. (Mrs. J. V. Bigford)
Below: Four Seattle natives who flew for VMSB-235: (l. to r.) Jack Bigford, Terry Dalton, Blackie Graham and Stan Grunland (KIA). (Mrs. J. V. Bigford)

Above: North American Mitchell bombers (B-25s) equipped several Marine squadrons that were first dispatched to the SWP early in 1944. Designated PBJs by the Marines, they operated first from the Treasury Islands, Green Island, and then Emirau, flying both day and night missions against targets on New Britain and New Ireland. Shown here at "Bombs Away!" is VMB-413. (USMC)

Below: Along with the standard flexible nose gun, this PBJ mounted a pair of fixed .50s protruding from the glass nose and dual two-gun packs on either side of the fuselage. It was assigned to VMB-413. The crew is: (back row, l. to r.) Lt. George Knauf, Lt. Col. Andrew Galatain, CO, Lt. Robert Cox, (kneeling, l. to r.) Sgts., Leo Gervis, Paul McCastland, and Michael Parina. (Author's collection)

Specially modified Lockheed PV-1 Venturas made their appearance in the SWP as Marine night fighters in late 1943 with VMF(N)-531. Flying intruder missions, they ranged over Japanese held islands, hounding the enemy at night. Left: CHLOE was the aircraft of CO, Col. Frank Schwable, and the plane was credited with four kills. (MNA) Below: GERTIE THE GOON, Maj. John Harshberger's plane, displays the Ventura's lethal armament, eight fixed forward firing guns. (MNA)

A gaggle of 13th Air Force P-38 aces pose in February 1944: Back row (l. to r.): Henry Meigs, 6 kills; George Chandler, 5; and Truman Barnes, 5. Bottom, kneeling (l. to r.) Bill Harris,15.5 victories; and Tom Walker, 6. All were with the 339th Squadron, 347th Fighter Group, and all survived combat. (George Chandler)

Japanese fighter pilots on Rabaul pose for a newspaper reporter early in 1944. (L. to r.) Takashi Kaneko, Masajiro Kawato, unknown Asahi war correspondent, and Yoshinobu Ikeda. Rabaul was reduced, isolated and bypassed, and with the Allied advance through the Carolines to the Marianas, no further aircraft replacements reached them. Still these and a few other pilots, with a handful of worn aircraft, continued to resist. (Y. Ikeda via Henry Sakaida)

Early in 1944 13th Air Force units were making a methodical transition to Lockheed P-38s. Above: One of the remaining Warhawks of the 44th Squadron, 18th Fighter Group over Sterling Island, 1st Lt. John Roehm at the controls. He claimed kills in both the P-40 and P-38. (Don Anderson)
Below: "Doc" Warrick by Bob Westbrook's 44th Squadron Lightning, showing 11 kill flags in April 1944. (Don Anderson)

By early 1944 the older model Lightnings began to be replaced by new versions with NMF in both 5th and 13th Air Forces. Above: Don Anderson, 44th Squadron, 18th Fighter Group and his RITA. (Don Anderson)

Below: A shiny new P-38J of the 44th in the Treasury Islands. The pylons under the center wing sections are for the attachment of auxilliary fuel tanks or bombs. (Don Anderson)

A pair of flying legends confer. Maj. Tom McGuire (left) and Charles A. Lindbergh discuss technical issues related to the P-38 Lightning. "The Lone Eagle" volunteered to assist both AAF and Marine units in the task of improving the capability of the P-38 and the F4U Corsair. Lindy flew 50 missions with those services in 1944. On 28 July 1944, over Western N.G., the 42 year-old civilian adviser became involved in an encounter with Japanese aircraft and was credited with downing a Mitsubishi Ki-51 Sonia. McGuire was the leading ace of the 475th Fighter Group and was later killed over the Philippines. (Bill Hess)

A New Guinea based B-25J of the 345th Bomb Group bears their highly distinctive nose and tail markings. They called themselves the "Air Apaches." (Ernie McDowell)

312th Bomb Group crews were devotees of nose art for their Douglas A-20G Havocs. Left to Right, Top to Bottom: READY TEDDY, MIS-A-SIP, MISS BEHAVEN, RAMAPO RATTLER, QUEEN O' HEARTS, RIDIN'HIGH. (Author's collection)

25

Allied SWP forces included a growing number of British Commonwealth units in 1944. Above: No. 14, 16 and 24 Squadrons, RNZAF flew the F4U-1D Corsair. This one carried a pair of different sized drop tanks. (Author's collection)
Below: A Mark VIII Spitfire of No. 457 Squadron RAAF on Morotai bearing yet another variation in the tiger shark design. (Author's collection)

As the Allies advanced northwest through New Guinea, they took over Japanese airfields or, working engineering miracles, quickly created new ones. Above: Aviation engineers fashioned this aircraft carrier-like layout on tiny Middleburg Is. late in August 1944, and 13th Air Force units were ordered forward from the Solomons. (NARS)
Below: No sooner had the fighters arrived than the Japanese conducted a night bombing that destroyed a pair of P-38s. (NARS)

CHAPTER 2

BATTERING THE MANDATES
AND THE REDUCTION OF TRUK

The Caroline Islands, part of the Micronesian Archipelago, had been one of Japan's earliest Pacific conquests, seized in World War I and later awarded by a League of Nations mandate. The vast stretch of islands and atolls measure over 2,500 miles east to west and one thousand miles in depth. Although the mandate forbid any military use of the new territory, the Japanese ignored the provision and set about a 20-year fortification program, creating airfields, supply depots, and naval facilities. Any Pacific advance by the Allies had to contend with this defensive network.

Early in 1944, Allied shore-based aircraft began to bring the Carolines under attack from the newly-won Gilbert Islands. U.S. Navy carrier task forces were growing in size and power, and employing amphibious warfare lessons learned in the SWP and Gilberts. Admiral Chester Nimitz, commander In chief Pacific Fleet (CINCPAC), struck north at the Marshall Islands taking Kwajalein and Eniwetok in January and February 1944. Supporting these operations, Task Force 58 thrust boldly at what was considered Japan's Pearl Harbor — Truk — on 17 February.

Emboldened by a lack of response from the Japanese main battle fleet, burgeoning U.S. Navy carrier forces raided with impunity along the periphery of the Empire's buffer zone through the first half of 1944. Truk was struck again on 29-30 April and struggled to defend itself. From this point onward, Truk was ignored by the Navy and left to be abused by periodic air raids of shore-based bombers. The once vaunted bastion had been bypassed and relegated to the back water of the Pacific war.

September landings in the Western Mandates at Palau were bravely contested by the Japanese garrison, but unsupported by air or naval forces. The Carolines were thus surrounded, subdued, and/or isolated.

After seizure of the Gilbert Islands, its air defense was provided by three squadrons of the 7th AF. Above, left: RACKER II and her pilot, Capt. Jim Carlyle, downed a pair of Vals in the predawn of 24 December 1943. With crew chief, Sgt. Phil Wall they contemplate the installation of a bulbous 175-gallon auxiliary tank. Right: 2nd Lt. Bill Eustis and his P-39Q, ITCHY BITCH, got a few holes in the tail from a Zeke over Mili. Below: An interesting view of the innards of a P-39Q under maintenance on Makin. The rear cavity housed the Allison 12-cylinder liquid cooled engine. The 37 mm cannon that fired through the prop hub, and the ammunition feed mechanism are forward of the cockpit. The Q-model also had a pair of .50 cal. machine guns in the nose over the cannon and one each in under-wing pods. These Makin-based P-39s were all from the 72nd Fighter Squadron. (All photos author's collection)

Low-level Liberators of VB-108 attack Japanese shipping in Kwajalein Atoll on 12 January 1944. This is the view from a PB4Y-1 left waist gun window. (NARS)

F/O Felix Scott in P-39Q, TEXAS ED, SN 42-19547, 46th Fighter Squadron, patrolled high over Makin on the night of 15 January 1944 and spotted a Japanese Nell in the island searchlights. He dove on the intruder and shot it down, one of the rare night kills for a day fighter. (Author's collection)

Several new aircraft carriers had joined the Pacific fleet by early 1944 in time for attacks on the Marshall Islands, next on the Allied invasion list. Above: An Avenger of VC-7 from *Manila Bay CVE-61*. (NARS)

Japanese air units in the Marshalls battled USN Task Force 58 as it made pre invasion strikes on Maloelap, Kwajalein and Wotje late in January 1944. Here an F6F from *Belleau Wood's* VF-24 scrambles even as the fleet is under attack. The black puffs indicate exploding AA fire. (MNA)

The thoroughness of Task Force 58 carrier strikes on the Marshalls is apparent in this recon view of Roi Island, Kwajalein Atoll, 29 January 1944. The smaller plumes of smoke are from individual aircraft and the large one is an oil storage fire. This photo was taken from a VT-6 Avenger. (MNA)

The invasion of Kwajalein and Eniwetok Atolls began on 31 January 1944. Close fire support was rendered by a swelling mass of surface ships. Their bombardment was directed by Vought Kingfishers like these OS2Us, the entire detachment from BB *South Dakota*. (Author's collection)

Ens. W.H. Hile of VF-51 crashed his F6F during landing on *San Jacinto* CVL-30. He survived to fly and fight another day. (USN)

Truk Lagoon, a major Imperial Navy fleet anchorage, supply base, and staging point for Japanese offensive operations in the South Pacific, was in the heart of the Carolines. As U.S. forces invaded the Gilberts and Marshalls of the Eastern Carolines, it became necessary to neutralize Truk. The first strike, on 17-18 February 1944, was conducted by four aircraft carriers. Above: The light cruiser *Katori*, first hit from the air, was later sunk by surface vessels. (MNA)
Below: The seaplane base at Dublon burns. Although Japanese counter attacks managed to torpedo but not sink *Intrepid*, they lost over 200 aircraft in the air and on the ground. (MNA)

Japanese warships in Truk Lagoon maneuvered furiously to avoid bombs and torpedoes. DD *Fumizuki,* seen here with an Avenger overhead, survived, but the Japanese lost three light cruisers, three destroyers, a seaplane tender, and a submarine tender. (NARS)

Lt. George Blair, a member of *Essex* 's VF-9, had taken several hits while dueling with defending Zekes, and his Hellcat went down inside Truk Lagoon. Other members of his squadron summoned help. An OS2U-3 Kingfisher from cruiser *Baltimore* , piloted by Lt. (jg) Denver Baxter, landed in the choppy waters under fire from ships and shore batteries. Chief Petty Officer Ruben Hickman pulled the wounded Blair aboard. With covering fire from VF-9 Hellcats, Baxter managed a tricky take-off and heroic rescue. They are seen here being recovered by *Baltimore* . (NARS)

Left: Lt. (jg) Alex Vraciu was already an ace with *Enterprise's* VF-6 when he downed three Zekes and a Rufe over Truk. He returned for a second tour of combat with VF-16 and ended his combat with 19 victories, including six in the "Marianas Turkey Shoot." (Author's collection)

On board carrier *Essex* Lt. (jg) Louis Menard (top) demonstrates one of his 17 February 1944 encounters over Truk. Below is Lt. (jg) Howard Hudson. Both VF-9 flyers scored, Menard claiming a pair of Kates and a pair of Petes, while Hudson downed a Kate. Both finished the war as aces, Menard with eleven victories and Hudson with five. (NARS)

The 45th Squadron, 15th Fighter Group flew missions against Japanese bases in the Marshall Islands from Makin. Here are a pair of its P-40N aircraft. Above: 1st Lt. Art Bridge (right) and his crew chief, Sgt. Jack Ward, inspect MISS CAPPY, armed with under-wing 500-pounders and a belly tank. (Author's collection)
Below: Maj. Gordon Hyde, 7th Fighter Command of 7th Air Force, flew with the 45th. The mission symbols, denoted by bombs and the Japanese victory flag, belong to the plane, flown by several pilots. This unit chose to paint their Warhawks a sand color, for a near perfect blend with the coral runways. The 45th experimented with 1,000 lb. bombs and 2.75 inch rockets against Japanese islands. (Author's collection)

Mili Island, in the Japanese-held Southern Marshalls, had a highly developed airdrome. It was attacked by carrier strikes, and after the adjacent Gilbert Islands were invaded, it was pounded relentlessly by both fighters and bombers of the 7th Air Force and Marines. By-passed and never invaded, it was already pockmarked by bombs this severely by March 1944. (USAF)

U.S. Navy fast carriers struck the Western Carolines on 30-31 March 1944 hitting shipping and installations in the Palau Islands.
Above: Japanese ships blaze from bomb hits. (MNA)
Below: A freighter draws the attention of VB-10, a bomb having just landed off its port side. (MNA)

An oil leak coats this VB-10 Dauntless and crew, but they managed to get back aboard *Enterprise* after raiding Yap Island. (MNA)

Left: A VF-16 Hellcat made a hard landing on *Lexington* CV-16, tangled with the barrier, nosed over, finally slammed to the deck, then broke its back. (NARS)

Truk was hit for a second time on 29-30 April 1944 by a strike force of no less than 12 aircraft carriers. Above: Dauntless SBDs of VB-16 roll into a strafing run over Ulalu Is., following bombing attacks. (NARS)
Below: As the naval base at Dublon burns, ships in the harbor await their fate. Three freighters were sunk along with some 20 lighters. (NARS)

Truk's Moen airfield as viewed from the cockpit of Lt. Cdr. J.D. Ramage's SBD on 29 April 1944. VB-10 was one of several squadrons that bombed and strafed the complex. A pair of Bettys burn while two more can be seen on a taxiway (left). Some twin-engine aircraft protected by revetments (right) survived the onslaught, but 60 of all types were destroyed on the ground. (MNA)

American aircraft losses over Truk in April 1944 amounted to 22, mostly from intense AA. Above: This VF-2 Hellcat returned to *Hornet* despite incredible flak damage. (NARS)
Below: An SBD-5 of VB-16, still carrying its bomb load, passes Dublon Is. on the second day of the raid. (MNA)

Reinforcement aircraft had been supplied to Truk after the February 1944 attack. They did not prevent nor minimize the damage caused by the April strike. Above: Navy fighters shot down 49 Zekes including this one. (NARS)
Below: A handful of attackers reached the fleet, like this torpedo carrying Nakajima B6N seen over the bow of *Lexington*, but they caused no damage. The Jill crashed moments later, its crew apparently dead or too wounded by AA to release the under-slung torpedo. (NARS)

VB-16 SBD-5s approach *Lexington* in April 1944 with tail hooks already lowered. (NARS)

A VF-29 Hellcat crash-landed on *Cabot* in April 1944. Deck crews douse the potential fire with foam. (USN)

Above: An April 1944 display of air power on Majuro in the Marshalls includes Navy Catalina flying boats, Hellcats of VF-39, Marine Avengers, and a Curtis Commando transport. (MNA)
Below: This VF-15 Hellcat from *Essex* got its tail badly mangled during a Marcus Is. raid on 20 May 44 but it managed a "no flaps" landing. (NARS)

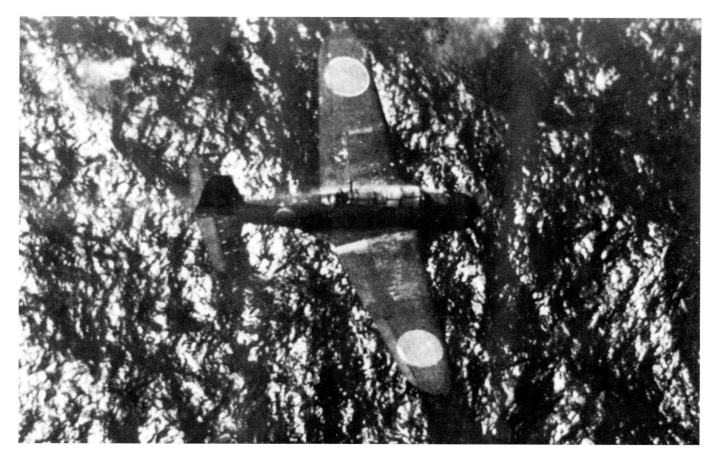

With the establishment of air bases in the Bismarck Sea region, Navy Liberators began probing deep into the Carolines. A luckless B5N Kate was encountered by a VB-109 aircraft and destroyed near Truk. (NARS)

A G4M Betty falls prey to the crew of a long-range patrol bomber. Ens. Paul Barker's crew of VPB-115, in a PB4Y-1 Liberator, combined for the victory over the Carolines. (NARS)

Navy PV-1 Lockheed Vega Venturas began long-range patrol operations in 1944. This aircraft was a direct descendent of the venerable Lockheed Hudson. It was armed with five .50 cal. machine guns, one in the dorsal turret, a pair in the top turret, and a fixed pair in the nose which were fired by the pilot. Above: A trio of PV-1s from VB-140 lugs auxiliary under-wing drop tanks to extend range. (Ken Sanford)

Below: A Ventura crew led by Lt. Harry Stanford, VB-148, downed this Betty of the 761st Kokutai near Truk. Note the smoke streaming from the right wing, the beginning of a fire. (NARS via Jim Lansdale)

Above: A VB 109 Liberator flew a very low-level reconnaissance mission over Tinian and photographed these G4M Bettys destroyed by a previous raid. (NARS)

Below: Cdr. Norman Miller's PB4Y-1, THUNDER MUG, returned from a raid against Paluwat in the Carolines without hydraulics and ran off the end of the runway, and hit its nose on an embankment, dumping its Erco nose turret on the beach. (NARS)

B-25s of the 41st Bomb Group, based in the Gilberts, raided the Marshalls beginning in December 1943. Above: The cannon-carrying B-25G, LITTLE JOE, OF THE 820th Squadron over Maloelap. (NARS)
Below: This B-25D lost an engine and its hydraulics to flak over Mili and bellied in on Makin's PSP fighter strip. (Author's collection)

A 41st Bomb Group B-25 Mitchell is pictured very low over Wotje Is., the Marshalls, its bomb bay doors still open. Note the skeleton of a hangar (right) burned out by a previous raid. (NARS)

The Navy hunted Japanese submarines as enthusiastically as it did surface ships. A hunter-killer group of DDs and DEs teaming with *Hoggatt Bay* CVE-75, operating north of the Admiralty Islands, managed to sink seven subs in less than a month during May-June 1944. Here a TBM of VC-14 crashed on return to *Hoggatt Bay* and is being man-handled into position. (MNA)

Left: The Liberator-equipped 30th Bomb Group arrived in the Central Pacific late in 1943 and flew strikes progressively from the Ellice, Gilbert, and Marshall Islands. The missions of this and other 7th Air Force heavy bomber units were beyond the range of AAF fighter escort. INCENDIARY SUE, a B-24J, SN 42-72991, shown here with ground crew on Kwajalein, had claimed three enemy aircraft by its 24th mission. (NARS)

Below: Truk's importance diminished after the Navy had administered two punishing carrier attacks. As the Allies moved north, Truk was bypassed and left in isolation. Heavy bombers of the 7th Air Force and Navy patrol squadrons maintained a watch on the base, conducting periodic raids. Here MADAME PELE, a B-24J of the 11th Bomb Group, retires after one such visit. (NARS)

CHAPTER 3

BATTLE OF THE PHILIPPINE SEA

The Marianas Islands of Saipan and Tinian had long been outposts of the Japanese Empire and constituted major links for supply, maintenance, and communications. The U.S. protectorate of Guam had been quickly added to this military structure when it was seized in the early days of the Pacific war. The Allied approach to the Marianas not only menaced the Philippines to the west, but it was a dagger pointing directly at the heart of the Japanese home islands.

In the days preceding the invasion of Saipan, 15 CVs and CVLs of Admiral Marc Mitscher's Task Force 58 struck Japanese bases in the Carolines. Then they turned their attention to neutralizing enemy forces in the Marianas in anticipation of D-Day, 15 June 1944.

The Japanese Combined fleet, absent from any major Pacific engagements for most of 1943, had been licking its wounds. However, the threat posed by the invasion of the Marianas could not be ignored. Most of Japan's existing carrier divisions, reequipped with new aircraft but largely untested air crews, sortied into the Philippine Sea. Japanese air units from nearby shore bases also mustered for a major confrontation with the U.S. Navy.

The Battle of the Philippine Sea involved more warships than had contested at Midway. The Japanese task force had nine carriers with over 430 aircraft embarked, with another 500-plus shore-based aircraft supporting the attack. As in Coral Sea and Midway, the two navies would not come close enough to engage in surface combat. The contest would be waged by the air fleets of both sides.

The Japanese sent successive waves against Task Force 58 on 19 June 1944, causing no appreciable damage and losing over 400 aircraft in the process. American flyers called it, "The Marianas Turkey Shoot." That afternoon, shadowing U.S. submarines torpedoed and sank Japanese aircraft carriers *Taiho* and *Shokaku*. Near sunset, aircraft from Task Force 58 located and attacked the retiring Japanese fleet sinking carrier *Hiyo* and damaging *Zuikaku* and *Junyo*. An additional 65 Japanese aircraft were lost in defense of the fleet or went down with their carriers.

U.S. combat losses for the two days were 39 aircraft and might have been far greater. In an unprecedented wartime decision, Task Force 58 turned on its lights to assist in the recovery of its returning aviators. Despite this, operational losses were 88 planes, many running out of fuel as a result of the long pursuit and a return in the dark.

The results for the Japanese were devastating. Despite the heroic effort of its naval air crews, the Marianas fell. The Imperial Navy remained a formidable force but one that had become dangerously deficient in aircraft carrier capability.

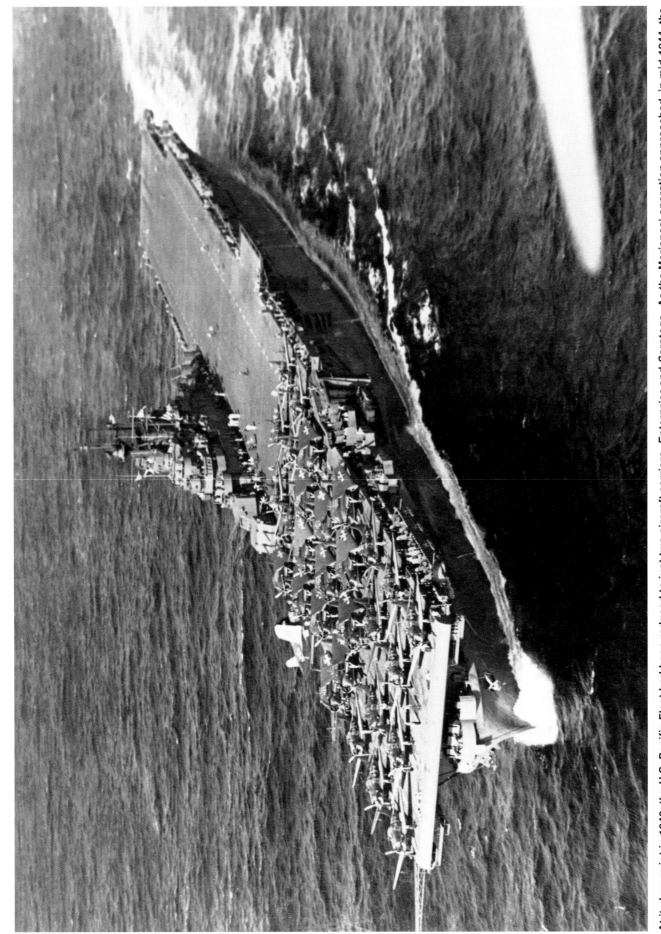

At its low point in 1942, the U.S. Pacific Fleet had been reduced to just two aircraft carriers, *Enterprise* and *Saratoga*. As the Marianas' operation approached, in mid-1944, the fast carrier force numbered 15. America's industrial capability in shipbuilding was one of the miracles of World War II. One of the new *Essex* class carriers, *Intrepid* CV-11, is seen here underway with Air Group 6 aboard in January 1944. (USN)

New and/or improved aircraft joined the fleet to outfit the armada of new carriers. Above: The Curtiss SB2C Helldiver began to displace the Douglas Dauntless in 1944. Nearly twice the weight of the SBD, the Helldiver was known as "The Beast". It had a greater bomb load and more fire power, but less range than the SBD. Shown here is a VB-1 Helldiver crossing the wake of *Yorktown* CV-10. (Bill Hess)
Below: A late model Grumman F6F-3 Hellcat, from VF-15 off *Essex,* is seen toting a 150 gal. long-range auxiliary drop tank. (Bill Hess)

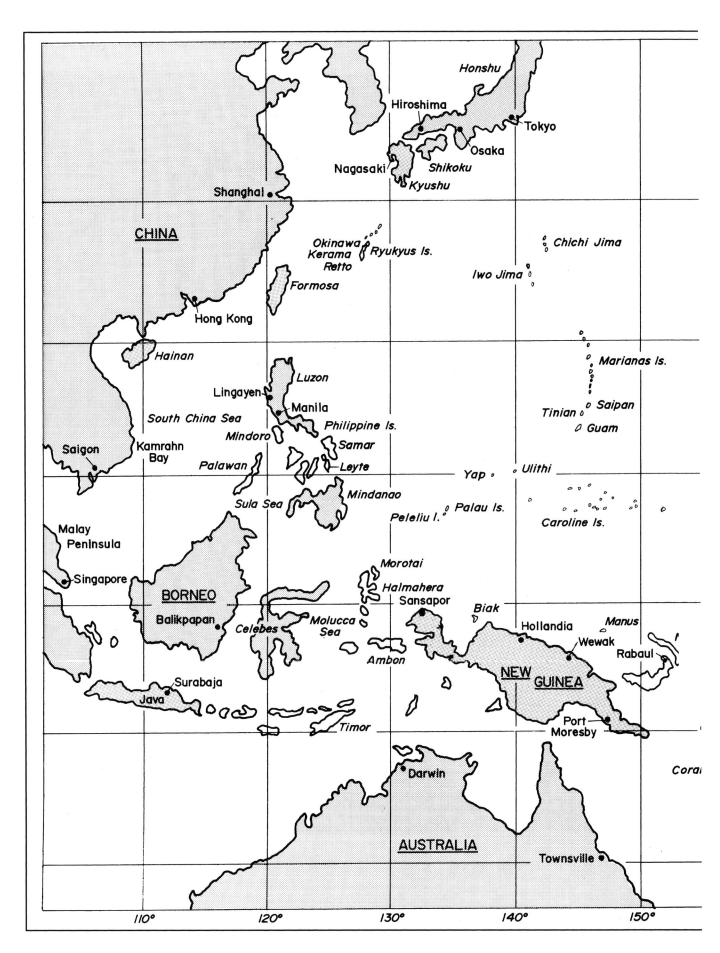

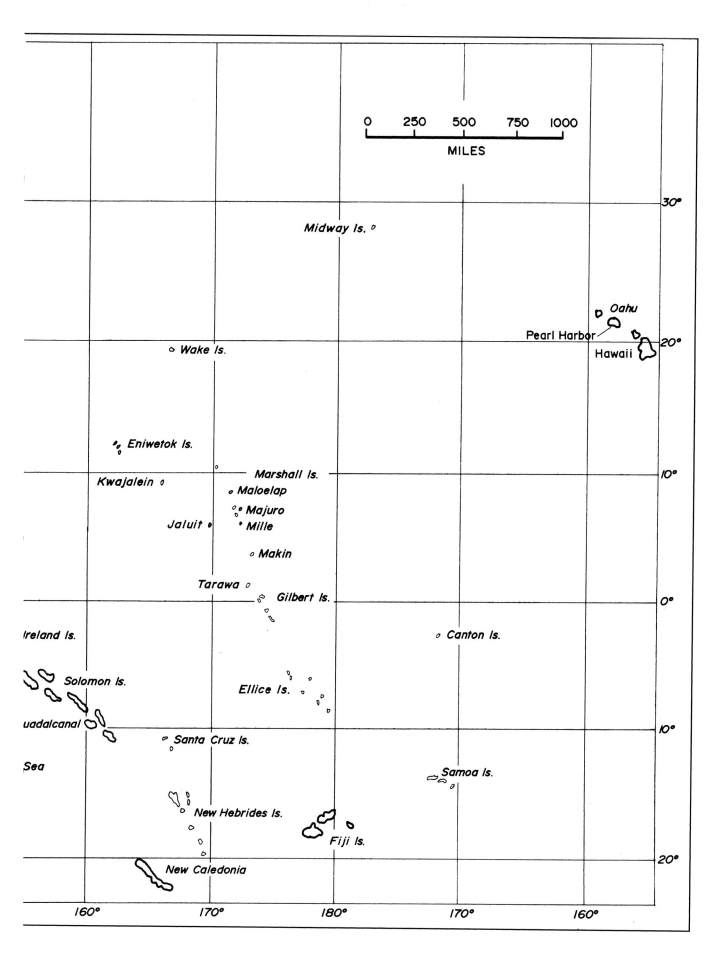

MILES

Midway Is. ◦

Oahu
Pearl Harbor
Hawaii

◦ Wake Is.

Eniwetok Is.

Marshall Is.

Kwajalein ◦

◦ Maloelap

◦ Majuro

Jaluit ◦

• Mille

◦ Makin

Tarawa ◦

Gilbert Is.

Canton Is.

Ireland Is.

Solomon Is.

Ellice Is.

uadalcanal

Santa Cruz Is.

Sea

Samoa Is.

New Hebrides Is.

Fiji Is.

New Caledonia

160° 170° 180° 170° 160°

30°
20°
10°
0°
10°
20°

Seen in the VT-16 ready room on Lexington prior to the assault on the Marianas are, foreground (l. to r.): Lt. Cdr. Robert H. Isely, squadron CO, Lt. (jg) Paul Dana, and Lt. Norman Sterrie. In the first use of rockets against ground targets, Isely led a low-level attack on Saipan's Aslito Airfield on 13 June 1944. Intense, accurate Japanese AA shot down and killed Isely and Dana and their crews. Aslito was later renamed Isely. Sterrie, on his second tour of combat, took command of the squadron. (USN)

On 13 June 1944 Lt. Cdr. William Martin led his VT-10 from *Enterprise* in a strike to soften up Japanese defenses on Saipan. His TBF-1C took a direct hit from AA and all three crewmen were blown from the aircraft. Martin's chute barely opened before he hit the water, and he never again saw his gunner and radioman. Despite being shot at from shore, Martin worked his way across a reef to the open sea, inflated his life raft, used his parachute as a sea anchor, and began using his signal mirror to attract Navy aircraft. A Curtiss SOC-3 from cruiser rescued him. Martin (center), and his two lost crewmen Wesley Hargrove and Jerry Williams, posed for this photo before the Saipan event. (Bill Balden)

Left: F6F-3 Hellcats of VF-8 prepare to sortie from Bunker Hill CV-17 on Saipan's D-day, 15 June 1944. (MNA)

Above: Japanese units from Truk, including Yokosuka D4Y Judys, reinforced the Marianas as invasion appeared imminent and Truk seemed destined to be left in the wake of the war. An excellent torpedo bomber of late design, a few Judys also served aboard the remaining Japanese aircraft carriers that engaged Task Force 58. (NARS)

Below: Many Japanese fighters never got into the air in the Marianas, due to bombing and strafing attacks or lack of fuel. This Mitsubishi Zeke 21 of the 261st Kokutai, being examined by U.S. soldiers on Saipan, appears relatively undamaged. The folding wing tip was standard for carrier based versions of the A6M. (NARS)

53556 A C

Left: As the Japanese Mobile Fleet advanced toward its historic engagement with the U.S Navy in June 1944, it dispatched scouts. This one a Jake, was spotted on 18 June 1944 by a flight of Hellcats from *Hornet*'s VF-2. Lt. (jg) Robert Shackford was credited with downing the float plane some 200 miles west of the fleet. Another *Hornet* aircraft took this photo of the action as Shackford's much faster F6F overtook and passed the doomed float plane. (NARS)

Japanese aircraft from the Mobile Fleet's four carriers and shore-based units attacked the U.S. Fifth Fleet in successive waves on 19 June 1944. Above: A Hellcat from VF-1, Lt. (jg) William Moseley in the cockpit, launches from *Yorktown.* He scored victories over two Zekes in the battle. An ace, Moseley was killed in action a few weeks later. VF-1 claimed 37 Japanese aircraft in the "Marianas Turkey Shoot." (NARS)

An F6F-3 from *San Jacinto*'s VF-51 aloft with 150 gal. drop tank. VF-51 claimed 7 1/2 kills on 19 June 1944. (NARS)

A VF-16 Hellcat lands aboard *Lexington* off Saipan on 19 June 1944. VF-16 downed 46 Japanese attackers. (USN)

The Mobile Fleet retired on 20 June 1944, pursued in the Philippine Sea by aircraft from the U.S. Fifth Fleet. The attack was launched late in the day and found the Japanese some 300 miles to the northwest. Returning in the dark, many planes became lost or ran out of fuel. Above: Avengers of VT-15 prepare to launch from *Essex.* (USN)
Below: Curtiss SB2C-1 Helldivers from *Yorktown*'s VB-1. Eight Helldivers were lost in combat and 33 others failed to reach their carriers (largely due to a lack of fuel), a disproportionate share of total Navy losses of 97 on 20 June. (USN)

Norman Sterrie (center) and his Avenger radioman, Klingbeil (left) and gunner, Jack Webb (right). Sterrie led six VT-16 Avengers in the 20 June 1944 dusk attack on Japanese carriers winning his third Navy Cross. One of the TBFs was downed by a Zeke and two others ditched after running out of fuel on the long return. Three made it back to the fleet. Sterrie landed in the dark after logging more than five hours. (Norman Sterrie)

Flying SBD dive bombers, Lt. Hal Buell was a veteran of the Battle of the Coral Sea and other early carrier actions. On a second tour of combat, he flew Curtiss SB2C bombers with VB-2 from *Hornet* CV-12. In the attack on the Japanese fleet, 20 June 1944, his plane took a direct flak hit, but he nursed it back to the fleet for a night crash-landing on *Lexington.* A Navy Cross winner, he retired from the Navy in 1962. (USN)

Cdr. James D. "Jig Dog" Ramage, led VB-10 flying from *Enterprise* during the critical battles of mid-1944. He retired from the post-war Navy with the rank of Rear Admiral. (Barrett Tillman)

Cdr. William A. Dean, led VF-2 on a pair of deployments from November 1943 to September 1944. Flying from *Hornet* CV-12, Fighting Two scored 43 kills in the Marianas Turkey Shoot, with Dean — an 11-victory ace — getting two Zekes. VF-2 had a total of 248 claimed victories, losing seven pilots. (USN)

Cdr. Dave McCampbell of Air Group 15, from *Essex* CV-9. VF-15 was high scoring squadron for the Turkey Shoot with 68 1/2 kills. McCampbell personally got five Judys and two Zekes in two sorties. He later recalled downed Japanese aircraft represented by, "many fires and oil slicks on the water closely strung in nearly a direct line along the track of the raid for a distance of ten to twelve miles." (NARS)

Vice Admiral Marc A. Mitscher, carrier tactician supreme, led the U.S. Navy's growing fast carrier forces in 1944. This famous unit was initially designated Task Force 58. (Author's collection)

Tinian Island, within sight of Saipan, was invaded on 24 July 1944 and is seen here below a TBM-1C Avenger of VC-11, *Nehenta Bay* CVE-74. Escort carriers provided the day-to-day close support for ground forces ashore in the Marianas. (MNA)

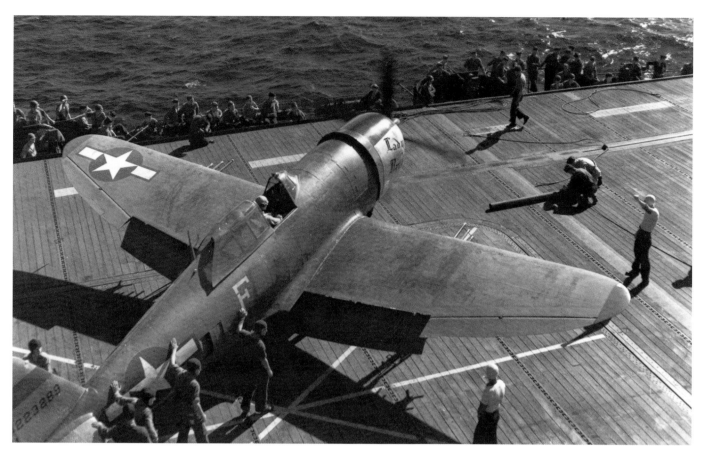

As Navy carrier forces moved on from the Marianas, the AAF moved in to provide an air garrison. Above: The 19th Squadron, 318th Fighter Group, 7th Air Force, was ferried to Saipan by the *Natoma Bay* CVE-62. Here a Republic P-47D-15-RA Thunderbolt, LADY RUTH, taxis toward the catapult on 23 June 1944. (NARS)

Below: The 318th's 333rd Fighter Squadron P-47s were catapulted off *Sargent Bay* CVE-83. Despite Navy assurances, the Army pilots were apprehensive about launching them and six tons of loaded aircraft. However, none crashed. (NARS)

The 318th Fighter Group set to work immediately, flying CAP and supporting infantry forces in the Marianas. Above: Capt. John Vogt and Lt. Bill Loflin (later KIA), 19th Squadron, verify the bomb line prior to a ground support sortie. The enemy was just a few miles from their base at Aslito Field. (Author's collection)

Below: 318th armorers used abandoned Japanese 250 lb. ordnance, until better stocks of bombs could be landed. (Author's collection)

Above: A P-47D of the 318th loaded and ready for a mission. Saipan and Tinian sorties were only minutes away from take-off at Aslito. (Author's collection)

Right: The tail of Lt. Wayne Kobler's 19th Squadron P-47 was found on Tinian near his grave where he was shot down by enemy AA. (Author's collection)

Above: The 6th Night Fighter Squadron introduced the Northrop P-61A Black Widow to Pacific combat operations on Saipan in June 1944. Until this point in time the AAF had not fielded an aircraft designed solely for the task of night combat. The P-61 packed a devastating four 20mm cannons in the nose. A factory installed top turret of four .50 cal. guns was removed in the field because of weight, buffet and flash-blinding considerations. The quad-20s were quite sufficient to the task. (Jim Alford)

Below: The Western Electric SCR-720 radar transmitter, night eye of the Black Widow, is uncovered for maintenance on Aslito. (Lew Sanders)

Above: The first confirmed night victory for the 6th Squadron, and for the P-61, was credited to MOONHAPPY, Lt. Dale Haberman, pilot, and F/O Ray Mooney, RO, east of Saipan on 30 June 1944. This team would claim three more kills. Note that the nose cone is plastic. (Author's collection)
Below: One of cartoonist Milt Caniff's beauties graced the P-61 of Capt. Mark Martin, 6th NF Squadron. In the last six months of 1944 the 6th downed eleven night raiders with two probables. (Author's collection)

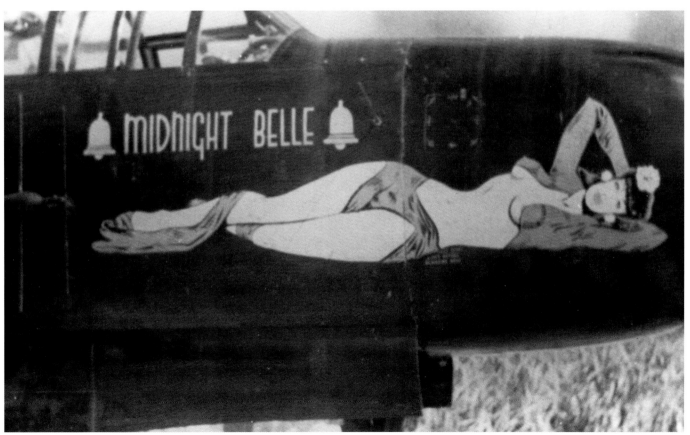

69

Guam was assaulted by amphibious forces on 21 July 1944, completing the seizure of the main Marianas islands. Hellcat night fighters of VMF(N)-534 quickly began operating from Orote Field on Guam. An F6F-3N is warming up. Its radar unit is in the bulging radome near the right wing tip. (USMC)

Aslito Airfield on Saipan became a mecca for Allied war planes. The F6F-3s in the foreground are from from VF-51. Center is a Northrop P-61 of the 6th Night Fighter Squadron, and in the distance are P-47 Thunderbolts of the AAF's 318th Fighter Group, and a row of Marine Consolidated 0Y-1 "Grasshoppers." (NAM)

Right: During the first carrier strike on the Philippines in late September 1944, Ens. Claude Plant of VF-15 downed two Aichi Vals over Mindanao. A few days later he crashed on return to *Essex* but was unhurt despite this "nose-up." On 12 September he was in a dogfight over Cebu and was seen to down a Zeke, but he failed to return. Plant's total score was 8.5 enemy aircraft. (MNA)

Below: TBM Avengers of VT-2 approaching *Hornet* during operations to invade the Palau Islands, 15 September 1944. (MNA)

Japanese garrison forces fought bitterly for the Palaus, and Marine units assisted with close support, using bombs and jellied gas (Napalm) against infantry in caves. VMF-114 arrived on Peleliu Is. with its Corsairs on 26 September 1944 and sometimes flew several missions a day, targets being only minutes away. (USMC)

A P-47 "Jug" of the 333rd Squadron, 318th Fighter Group stands on alert at Saipan, crew chief at the controls. There were few Japanese day raiders over the Marianas, yet the 318th bagged six before the end of the 1944. (Joe Maita)

Above: Flying from the newly seized Marianas, 11th Bomb Group B-24s reached out south to Truk and north to the Bonin Islands, the latter just 600 miles from Honshu. (NARS)

Below: Intercepting fighters on Iwo Jima, Bonin Is., damaged HOUSE OF BOURBON; a 30th Bomb Group B-24J, SN 42-100227 so badly that pilot 1st Lt. William Core had to crash-land in the Marianas. It was the last of 36 missions for this Lib, but her crew survived. (NARS)

As Japanese islands fell, 7th Air Force heavy bomber units advanced their attacks deeper into enemy territory. Above: DUMBO THE AVENGER, a B-24D, SN 42-72832, of the 25th Squadron, 11th Bomb Group displays its record on Guam. (Jim Crow)

Below: A phosphorous explosive on a Japanese AA shell misses a formation of 30th Bomb Group Liberators. Japanese AA gunners on by-passed islands remained dangerous. (Jim Crow)

UPSTAIRS MAID, B-24J,SM 42-109941

SWEET ROUTINE, B-24J, SN 44-40527

NIGHT MISSION, B-24J, SN 44-40532

BAT OUT OF HELL, B-24J, SN 42-73024

HELL FROM HEAVEN, B-24J, SN 44-40528

THE CAPTAIN AND THE KIDS, B-24J,SN 44-40518

30th Bomb Group Liberators featured some of the most exotic nose art in the Central Pacific. The unit advanced from Kwajalein to Saipan on 4 August 1944. Each bomb painted on the nose represents one mission. (Author's collection)

Boeing B-29 Superfortress bombers operating out of China had first raided Japan in July 1944. Thus the arrival of new B-29 units on Saipan in October 1944 posed a threat to the homeland that could not be ignored. Lacking any real long-range aircraft capability, the Japanese staged desperate day and night raids through the island chain to the Marianas. A series of attacks on 27 November 1944 destroyed four B-29s and damaged a dozen more. A strafing Zeke of the 252nd Naval Air Group, on a one-way suicide mission, dove into this Superfort. A Navy Catalina, to the far right, was considered unworthy of such attention. (USAF)

CHAPTER 4

THE BATTLE FOR LEYTE

The invasion of the Philippines — MacArthur's "return" — began at Leyte on 20 October 1944. For the Japanese and the Allies, Leyte became a crucible.

Despite Japanese reverses of 1942-43, the neutralization of the Carolines, and the loss of the Marianas, Imperial Navy Headquarters had retained the view that they could still win the war by bringing the U.S. Navy to a decisive ship-to-ship engagement. This unrealistic assessment was due partly to Japan's inherent faith in its own military superiority, never having lost a war, and a belief in its own propaganda. The pre-Luzon naval actions of 1944, according to Japanese news reports, were supposed to have dealt crippling blows to American carrier task forces.

The invasion armada off Leyte was, therefore, a lightning rod for the Japanese. It set in motion movement of the Combined Fleet in what was labeled the "Sho-go Plan," literally, "Victory Operation." One aspect of the strategy involved a new tactic, borne of desperation, Special Attack units. The first of these suicidal Kamikazes were assembled at airfields in the Philippines. Historically, the engagement transcended the 1916 Battle of Jutland in sheer numbers of ships. In its ferocity, the Battle for Leyte Gulf was unrivaled.

Elements of the Combined Fleet sortied from Japan, the Pescadores, and Singapore in a highly orchestrated operation. Vice Admiral Jisaburo Ozawa led a force of 17 ships south from Japan toward the Philippine Sea. It included four aircraft carriers but only 108 carrier aircraft, a measure of the severe depletion of experienced naval air crews. Admiral Takeo Kurita led an awesome surface force from the west, including the mightiest battleship ever built, *Yamato.* A second squadron, led by Vice Admiral Kiyohide Shima, passed through the Mindanao Sea to emerge through Surigao Straits at the bottom of Leyte Gulf.

The largest battle force (with Kurita) sailed through the Sibuyan Sea to emerge from San Bernardino Straits off Samar. On 24 October 1944, he was attacked and damaged, but not stopped, by submarines and Task Force 38 aircraft. Kurita's strategy was to apply a pincer on the thin-skinned invasion transports and their fleet of supporting escort carriers, destroying the Leyte landing, and confronting the U.S. fleet. Ozawa was nothing more than a decoy, intended to draw off the U.S. fast carriers.

Based on early reconnaissance and estimates of Japanese intentions, Admiral William Halsey, commanding Third Fleet, took the bait and pursued Ozawa. In doing so, Task Force 38's fast carriers, ranged beyond support of Leyte. Halsey had left a blocking force at Surigao Strait, but San Bernardino was unprotected. Ozawa's carrier force was located, brutalized by air attacks, then finished off by surface warships, losing all four carriers, all of its aircraft, and many escorting vessels. Air attacks, PT boats, and the blocking force devastated the Shima squadron, none of which reached Leyte Gulf.

However, Kurita with 23 warships surprised the CVEs, arrayed a few miles apart in units designated Taffy 1, 2, and 3. Japanese battleships, cruisers, and destroyers began what should have been a slaughter. Some of their largest caliber shells, 18-inch and 16-inch armor-piercing battleship rounds, passed directly through the hulls of U.S. ships. In one of those improbable miracles of warfare, the tenacious response by Taffy escort vessels and repeated attacks by CVE Wildcat and Avenger squadrons, disrupted Kurita's pursuit. The swarming defense, by relatively few aircraft, caused him to reflect that he must have stumbled near the U.S. fast carrier fleet.

Avenger pilots from the jeep carriers had few torpedoes but went after the Japanese with 500-pounders, then made wave-top runs to simulate torpedo attacks. Wildcat pilots made repeated low-level rocket and strafing passes at the enemy warships, continuing dry runs long after their ammunition had been expended. Fifty caliber machine guns had little effect on the heavily armored battleships and cruisers, but the attacks succeeded in disrupting navigation and fire control. Persistent bombing and strafing runs were pressed through a blizzard of flak. *Yamato* alone mounted 120 anti-aircraft guns. Those aircraft unable to recover on carriers flew to the barely operable 5th Air Force airstrips at Tacloban and Dulag on Leyte in search of fuel and ordnance.

After sinking one CVE, two DDs, and one DE, and damaging many other ships, Kurita's determination withered. He ordered a withdrawal back through San Bernardino Straits, but eventually many of his ships were hounded and sunk. Total Japanese losses for the overall battle were 57 warships, the U.S. Navy losing 14 to surface action and Kamikazes.

Operation Sho-go, which had all the ingredients for an American naval disaster, was another incredible victory for the U.S. Navy, one from which the Imperial Navy could never recover.

Pilots, man your planes!" sent these "Sun Downers" of VF-11 scrambling to their Grumman F6F Hellcats on *Hornet* CV-12, as operations to retake the Philippines began. During this second tour of combat duty VF-11 claimed 106 victories in less than four months. (Author's collection)

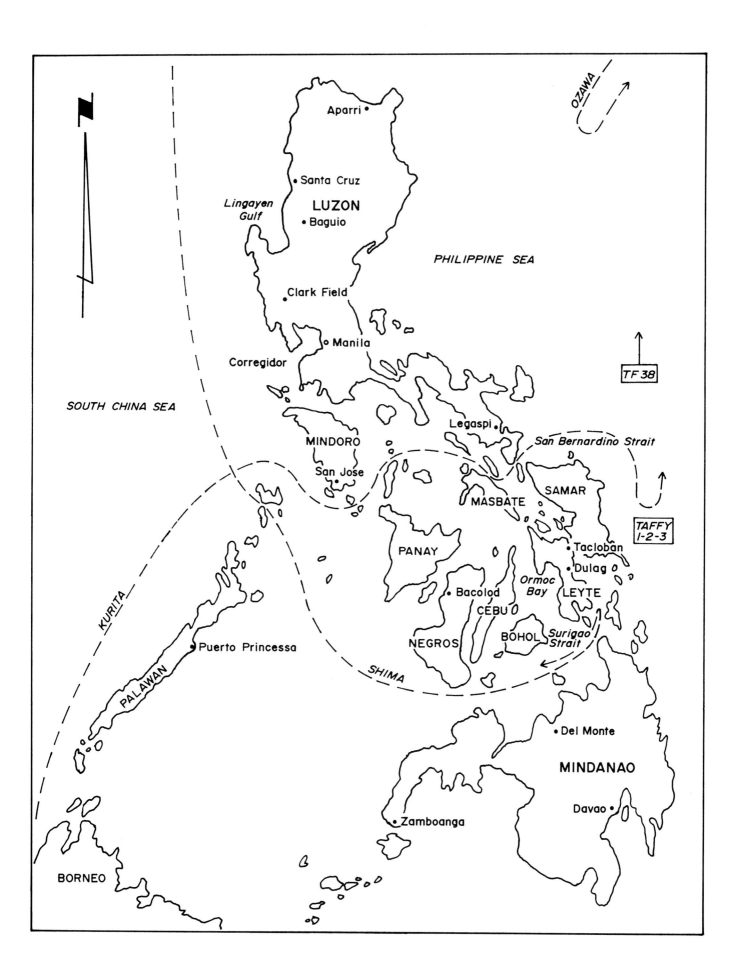

APARRI •

• Santa Cruz

Lingayen Gulf

LUZON

• Baguio

PHILIPPINE SEA

Clark Field

○ Manila

Corregidor

SOUTH CHINA SEA

MINDORO

Legaspi •

San Bernardino Strait

• San Jose

SAMAR

MASBATE

TAFFY 1-2-3

PANAY

• Tacloban

• Dulag

Ormoc Bay

• Bacolod

LEYTE

CEBU

KURITA

BOHOL

Surigao Strait

• Puerto Princessa

NEGROS

PALAWAN

SHIMA

• Del Monte

MINDANAO

• Davao

• Zamboanga

BORNEO

OZAWA

TF 38

79

Prior to the invasion of Leyte, fast carrier task forces attacked Japanese air bases in nearby islands. Above: An F6F of VF-29 prepares to launch from *Cabot* CVL-29 on the 10 October 1944 strike against Okinawa. (Author's collection)

Below: An SB2C-3 Helldiver of VB-7 from *Hancock* CV-19 flies below an overcast along the North coast of Formosa. It carries a search radar located in an under wing pod. The raids on Okinawa and Formosa cost the Japanese nearly 600 aircraft lost on the ground or in the air. The cost to U.S. Navy forces was 69 carrier aircraft. Many of the crew members were rescued by "Life Guard" submarines. (MNA)

Air strikes aagainst Luzon, Okinawa, and Formosa involved the first use of a carrier air group specifically trained and equipped for night operations. Above: VF(N)-41 F6F-5N Hellcats are seen in the foreground awaiting launching from *Independence* CVL-22. Radar is located in the bulge near the tip of the right wing. (MNA)
Below: VT(N)-41 flew similarly equipped TBM-1Ds, one of which is seen here on take-off. (USN)

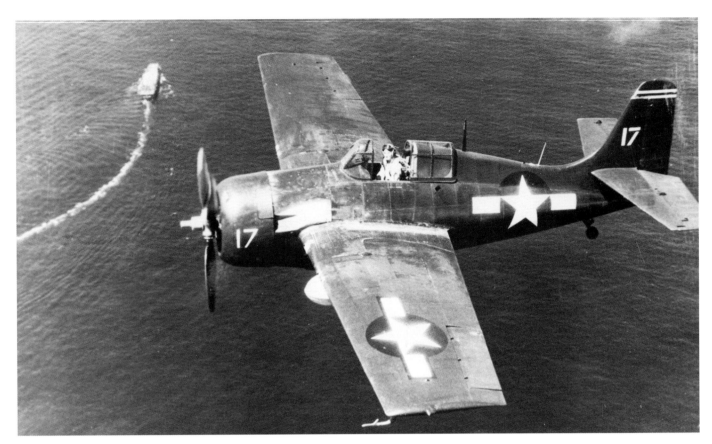

On 20 October 1944 MacArthur's Sixth Army made its amphibious landing on Leyte's east coast. It was supported by a vast fleet including 16 escort carriers. The CVEs were mostly equipped with TBM Avengers and FM-2 Wildcats (General Motors built versions of the Grumman TBF and F4F). Above: An FM-2 from *Santee's* VC-26 patrols over the fleet on D-Day. (USN)
Below: Ens. Ed Van Hise, VC-68, lost power on his Wildcat on take-off from *Fanshaw Bay*. He ditched successfully, got clear of his aircraft as the carrier steamed close by, and was rescued by a trailing DE. (MNA)

The Japanese reacted to the Leyte invasion with wave air attacks from shore bases against the fast carriers operating in the Philippine Sea. On 24 October 1944 the CAP of Task Force 38.3 downed dozens of attackers. However, one Judy slipped through the fighter screen and planted a bomb squarely on the flight deck of *Princeton* CVL-23. With fires raging, her CAP had to land aboard other carriers. Above: This VF-27 Hellcat, piloted by Lt. Carl Brown (5 kills this date) recovered on *Essex*. *Princeton*, marked by the trail of smoke on the horizon, eventually sank with a loss of over 140. (NARS)
Below: Crews of *Essex* work to pack their own and orphaned *Princeton* aircraft forward on the flight deck. (NARS)

Above: DE *Dennis,* part of the protective screen of "Taffy 3," races past *Kitkun Bay* toward the Japanese battle wagons. At this point in the action all ships are laying smoke screens to confuse the Japanese gunners. Like other ships of the screening force, *Dennis* boldly attacked the much larger Japanese force. She was damaged but survived. Two DDs and a DE from Taffy 3's screen were sunk as they fearlessly confronted the Japanese heavy weights. Kurita lost three heavy cruisers to a combination of ship and air attacks. (NARS)

Below: As Japanese salvos raise water spouts around *White Plains*, crews on *Kitkun Bay* CVE-71 work feverishly to launch their aircraft. An FM-2 of VC-5 is in the foreground, prop turning. (USN)

Taffy 3 was running for its life off Samar Island as the Japanese fleet of four BBs, six heavy cruisers, two light cruisers and 12 destroyers bore down. The CVEs could only muster 17 1/2 knots. Even the Japanese battleships could make 27. Above: *Gambier Bay* is straddled by naval shells as smoke screens were being laid. She was hit repeatedly and sank with the loss of over 130 crew members. (USN)

Right: *St. Lo* had avoided the rain of shells from Kurita's warships but came under attack from enemy aircraft. A Zeke from Luzon, piloted by Lt. Yukio Seki, ran the gauntlet of AA fire and crashed among Avengers that were being armed. Fires eventually touched off *St. Lo*'s stores and she sank with the loss of 114 crew members. Japanese gunners scored 14 hits on *Kalinin Bay* and four on *Fanshaw Bay*, but both survived the encounter. (NARS)

Above: An 8-inch Japanese cruiser shell has just penetrated the flight deck of *Kalinin Bay*, buckling her elevator and showering the deck with wood splinters, as crew members man a fire hose. (USN)
Below: Near misses from Kurita's warships send geysers over a wounded *Gambier Bay* (left), as *Kitkun Bay* makes smoke and runs. (USN)

Wildcats and Avengers from the CVEs hurled themselves at the Kurita's main force in Leyte Gulf with whatever ordnance was available until ammunition or sometimes fuel were exhausted, then made repeated dummy runs to disrupt navigation and gunnery on the Japanese warships. Above: The heavy cruiser, *Tone*, part of Adm. Kurita's main force, is viewed here by a TBM-1C Avenger of VC-81 from *Natoma Bay* CVE-62. Avenger pilots made repeated dummy torpedo runs distracting the Japanese from an efficient pursuit of the CVEs. (NARS)

Below: A *Sangamon* Hellcat pilot (one of the two escort carriers utilizing the F6F) buzzes a squadronmate who has ditched. (NARS)

Army aviation engineers had barely finished work on the runway at Tacloban, Leyte, when Wildcat and Avenger pilots from the hard-pressed CVEs sought refuge ashore. Their ships had either been lost, damaged or unable to conduct landing operations in the face the enemy menace. Above: TBMs and FM-2s are scattered about the air strip. (NARS)

Below: A *St. Lo* FM-2 managed to get some fuel and took off to make additional strafing runs on the Kurita force. An AAF crew (left) attempts to clear a wrecked aircraft. (NARS)

The 307th Bomb Group, dispatched from Noemfoor, found Kurita's battle force retiring through Mindoro Straits near Panay Island on 26 October 1944. Twenty-seven B-24s attacked the armada from about 10,000 feet. Above: The Japanese fleet maneuvers wildly to avoid the Liberator's rain of 1,000-pounders. (James Kendall)

Below: BB *Kongo* took a pair of hits on the bow but plows forward. BB *Yamato* also shrugged off one direct hit. The Japanese fleet threw up a torrent of AA, including the main batteries firing at the 307th still eight miles distant. The Japanese fire was so intense that three B-24s were downed and 14 were damaged. (James Kendall)

As the uneven struggle off Samar was being played out, Admiral Ozawa had led a force of 18 warships (including four aircraft carriers) from Japan to engage the U.S. Third Fleet and Admiral Mitscher's powerful fast carriers. The Ozawa "Northern Force" was a decoy, intended to draw U.S. carrier air power away from Kurita's battle force. The strategy succeeded, but Ozawa's ships paid a terrible price, eight being lost. Above: *Zuiho* sank under a rain of bombs and torpedoes on 25 October 1944 off Luzon's Cape Engano in the Philippine Sea. The camouflage design was intended to confuse enemy aerial scouts. (NARS)

Above: An *Enterprise* TBM-1C from VT-20 after the slaughter of Ozawa's fleet. The pilot was Lt. E.E. Rodenbourgh. It returned bearing severe flak damage on its right wing, made visible as the Avenger's wings are folded. (USN)
Below: SB2C-3 Helldivers of VB-20 from *Enterprise* returning to Third Fleet. Mitscher's carrier air groups sank all four carriers and a DD. Surface ships overtook and sank another three warships.(MNA)

Elements of the 5th Air Force's 49th Fighter Group arrived with their P-38s at Leyte's Tacloban airfield on 27 October 1944. The strip was already overcrowded, and rains fostered mud that created operational problems. However, the 9th Squadron immediately flew defensive patrols, scattering a small force of Vals and downing two. (USAF)

The Mitsubishi J2M Raiden (Thunderbolt) was a swift new fighter, encountered in combat for the first time over the Philippines. It was named "Jack" by the Allies. The 7th Squadron, 49th Fighter Group downed a pair of Jacks on 2 November 1944. (Ernie McDowell)

Task Force 38.4 was engaged in operations off Samar on 30 October 1944 when it came under intense attack from Japanese land-based aircraft including Kamikazes. Above: *Enterprise* was narrowly missed by a bomb off its port stern quarter. VF-20 Hellcats are in the foreground. (MNA)

Right: Sister ships were not so lucky. *Franklin,* and *Belleau Wood* were both hit by Cebu-based Zekes of the 1st Special Attack Corp, Hazakura Unit. *Belleau Wood,* seen here, controlled her fires, but along with *Franklin,* had to retire to Ulithi for major repairs. The two carriers suffered collective casualties of 142 killed and 110 injured. (MNA)

Scouting and searching for commerce deep into Japanese territory, Navy patrol bombers had "battle of the giants" encounters as shown on this and the facing page. Above: A PB4Y Liberator of VB-117 chases a Japanese H8K Emily near the Bonin Islands on 31 October 1944. (NARS)

Below: The Emily hugs the water as it is sprayed by the .50 caliber guns of the Lib. It was eventually downed. The Navy crew was led by Lt. Cdr. H.M. McGaughey, and this was one of five aerial kills for his crew. (NARS)

Above: On 22 November 1944, near the Celebes, Lt. A.Y. Bellsey's VPB-101 crew sighted a Kawanishi H6K Emily and set it afire. (NARS) Below: Backing off, they watched the doomed flying boat descend just prior to its crashing. (NARS)

The 475th Fighter Group arrived at Leyte on 3 November, 1944 and operated from the newly completed Dulag airstrip. Above: PUTT PUTT MARU was the P-38J of Col. Charles MacDonald, a charter member of the 475th who rose to command the group. He was credited with 27 victories. (Author's collection)
Below: FLORIDA CRACKER belonged to 9-victory ace, 1st Lt. Joe Forster, of the 432nd Squadron. (Bill Hess)

The ground war on Leyte was a grim slugging match which the Japanese were losing. Believing that they could still win, a massive reinforcement effort was undertaken from Manila. Starting on 9 November 1944, convoys of transports and escorts sailed for Ormoc on Leyte's west coast. They were attacked by AAF low-level bombers and later by carrier based aircraft, suffering heavy losses in men and ships, an effort that failed to save Leyte. Right: The landing ship, *Takatsu Maru,* weaves through near misses by 38th Bomb Group Mitchells but was eventually sunk. (NARS)

Below: A Japanese merchant ship avoids a string of bombs. The bow platform houses AA guns. (NARS)

Left: An Imperial Navy DE (possibly Type C, No. 11) attempts to outrun low-level 38th Bomb Group B-25s in Ormoc Bay on 10 November 1944. Note that the main forward turret and the midships AA battery gunner's (between the bridge and the stack) attention is directed to starboard, while the overhead Mitchell has approached from the stern. (NARS)

Below: A view of the the starboard beam shows direct hits amidships that sank this vessel. The rows of what appear to be white barrels toward the stern are depth charges. (NARS)

What may be DD *Naganami* sinks by the stern on 11 November 1944 55 miles northeast of Cebu enroute to Ormoc. She was attacked alternately by Task Force 38 and the 5th AF. (NARS)

A patrolling P-38 pilot from the 431st Squadron, 475th Fighter Group waves at the cameraman. Between early November and 7 December 1944, the 475th claimed 99 victories in air battles over Leyte and the nearby Visayan Islands. (Bill Hess)

Left: The 5th Air Force's top-scoring fighter pilots, Tom McGuire (left) and Dick Bong, teamed up for a short time on Leyte. Bong claimed his 40th and final victory, an Oscar near Negros Island, on 17 December 1944. Bong was then "ordered" home. McGuire, chasing Bong's record, continued scoring victories over the Philippines until achieving 38 kills. (Bill Hess)

Below: Tom McGuire's 431st Fighter Squadron P-38J with 25 kill flags. He was killed in action over Negros Island on 7 January 1945. McGuire attempted to engage an Oscar at low altitude and entered a turning stall from which he could not recover. (Bill Hess)

In the first days of November 1944, Task Force 38 applied pressure on Luzon's airfields, where aircraft reinforcements were arriving from Formosa and points north. Above: Air Group 14 from *Wasp,* with rocket equipped Hellcats in the foreground, prepares to sortie. (MNA)
Below: A VT-15 Avenger from *Essex* returns with a dead gunner. His body is being removed from the lower hatch. (USN)

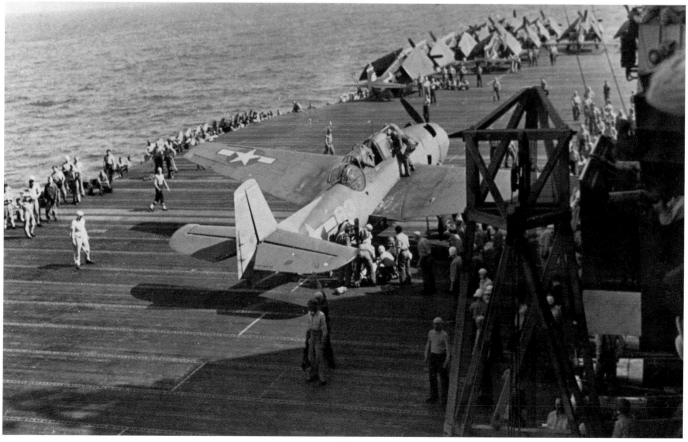

Above: A PB4Y-1 Liberator, with VPB-116 out of Tinian, overhauled and downed this Kawanishi H8K Emily in late November near the Bonin Islands. (USN)

Below:Training was often as hazardous as combat. As *Makassar Strait*, CVE-91 made its way toward the Pacific fleet, one of her FM-2 Wildcats landed hot (No. 5) and demolished a parked Wildcat (No. 9) before it plunged over the side. The VC-97 pilot was rescued by a DE. (USN)

Japanese attacks on the surface fleet were relentless. Above: A Zeke is seen in the gun camera view on a full deflection shot from Ens. Owen Miller's VC-81 FM-2 near Mindoro on 14 December 1944. He was providing CAP from *Natoma Bay*. VC-81 claimed 21 victories in the Philippines.(NARS)
Below: VC-4 FM-2s from *White Plains* on patrol. VC-4 claimed eight kills near the Philippines. (NARS)

Before the ground campaign for Leyte was over, MacArthur's forces leap-frogged across the Sibuyan Sea to take lightly defended Mindoro Island, landing on 15 December 1944. Five days later an airfield was ready and the 8th Fighter Group arrived from Morotai. Before they could land, the P-38s were vectored to an incoming Japanese air raid. Above: The 8th downed four Oscars and two Nicks, but the Lightning of Lt. Oran Anderson was hit and crashed. He survived. (NARS)
Below: A few nights later a Japanese bomber destroyed this P-38L-1 with a near direct hit. (NARS)

Above: The Lightning of 1st Lt William "Ken" Giroux, 36th Squadron, 8th Fighter Group. He was officially credited with ten victories and three probables. His final victory was an Oscar over Negros Is. (Bill Hess)
Below: A P-38L-5 of the 36th Squadron, 8th Fighter Group, was utterly destroyed in this crash-landing, but its pilot, Lt. Francis S. Ford, managed to stagger away. (AFM)

Above: P-38Ls of the 36th Squadron, 8th Fighter Group at Mindoro, P.I. in December 1944. (AFM)
Below: Capt. Robert DeHaven, 7th Squadron, 49th Fighter Group by his P-38L-5 on Leyte. DeHaven served three tours of combat with the 49th, flying the Curtiss P-40 from mid-1943 until mid-1944. On his second tour he flew the Lightning, scoring the last four of his 14 victories over the Philippines. He accumulated 272 combat missions into 1945. (Jim Crow)

Langley CVL-27, with Air Group 44 aboard, is seen here in heavy seas. She was part of Task Force 38 sailing in the Philippine Sea off Luzon when a killer typhoon was encountered on 18 December 1944. Three DDs capsized with heavy loss of life, and many other Third Fleet ships were damaged, but air operations against Luzon resumed the following day. (USN)

Heavy bombers from the 5th, 7th and 13th Air Forces supported the advance into the Philippines from Morotai and the Palaus. Above: An overly aggressive Japanese fighter pilot made a tail attack on this B-24 of the 307th Bomb Group, colliding with the left vertical stabilizer and then buckling the right wing, dooming all crew members. The incident took place over the Southern Philippines in November 1944. (NARS)

Below: Its "Bombs away!" over Cebu, for this Angaur, Paulau-based B-24M of the newly arrived 494th Bomb Group, 7th Air Force. Tail markings on SN 44-2056 are those of the 865th Squadron. (NARS)

On this and the following page are profiles of a few of the AAF and Navy aces whose Pacific combat careers came to a close, one way or the other, in 1944. All had outlived their luck.

A 20-victory ace with the 13th Air Force's 347th Fighter Group, Lt. Col. Robert Westbrook flew both the P-40 and P-38 from the Solomons to the Celebes. He was killed in action on 22 November 1944 over Makassar Strait while strafing enemy ships. He had been awarded the Distinguished Service Cross and many other decorations.(NARS)

1st Lt. Jay Robbins, began his Pacific combat service with the 80th Squadron, 8th Fighter Group in January 1943 in Bell P-39s. He soon transitioned to the Lockheed P-38 and eventually became CO of the 80th. By the end of his combat career in December 1944 he had scored 22 victories in 181 sorties. Awarded the Distinguished Service Cross and many other decorations, he retired as a lieutenanat general. (NARS)

Petty Officer Donald E. Runyon, one of the Navy's few non-officer pilots, flew with VF-6 from *Enterprise.* In the spirited battles of August 1942 near the Solomons Islands, he downed eight Japanese planes. Promoted to officer rank, Lt. Runyon later served another tour of combat in early 1944 with VF-18 aboard *Bunker Hill* CV-17, adding three more kills to his record. (MNA)

Lt. Cdr. Edward Outlaw, CO of VF-32 operating from *Langley* CVL-27, scored his sixth and final victory over Saipan on 11 June 1944. Here his plane captain, H.T. Sliper (left) poses with the skipper. (NARS)

Lt. Col. Tom Lynch saw his first action in a Bell P-400 in May 1942 with the 35th Fighter Group. He served for an extraordinary period in combat until killed in action while strafing Japanese luggers near Tadji, N.G. on 9 March 1944. He had 20 confirmed kills, all but one in the P-38. (NARS)

"Wayne" Morris, a genuine Hollywood movie star, volunteered for the Navy and flight training and became one of VF-15's 26 aces. Lt. Bert D. Morris, had seven victories. (USN)

Col. Neel Kearby had led the Republic P-47 Thunderbolt equipped 348th Fighter Group into combat. A Medal Of Honor winner, he racked up 22 kills in just six months of combat. After a dog fight near Wewak on 5 March 1944 he parachuted and died of his injuries. (NARS)

Hamilton "Mac" McWhorter first saw combat with VF-9 flying F4Fs from *Ranger* during the November 1942 invasion of North Africa. He continued with the unit as they transitioned to F6F Hellcats and went to Pacific combat aboard *Essex* in 1944. He scored ten victories in raids on Truk and other Central Pacific targets. He returned for a third tour of combat on *Randolph* CV-15 with VF-12, flying in the campaigns against Iwo Jima, Okinawa and Japan, and racking up two more victories. After serving in the postwar Navy he retired with the rank of commander. (NARS)

Lt. Charles Stimpson of VF-11, climbing down from his F6F-5 in November 1944. Six of his kills were from the first tour of VF-11 on Guadalcanal. When the squadron downed eighteen bandits near Formosa on 14 October 1944, Stimpson got five, and was awarded the Navy Cross. (Author's collection)

VF-15, flying Grumman Hellcats from *Essex* between June and November 1944, participated in most of the major aerial engagements of the Pacific war, downing 310 enemy aircraft, the highest USN score for a single tour of combat. The squadron suffered 20 losses. CO of Air Group 15, Cdr. David McCambell, eventually racked up 34 kills, tops for the USN, and was awarded the Medal of Honor. (NARS)

The Pacific war produced America's leading ace, Maj. Richard I. Bong, a farm boy from Wisconsin. He entered combat as a second lieutenant in November 1942 with the 35th Fighter Group and was soon transferred to the 9th Squadron, 49th Fighter Group for the balance of his Pacific duty. Bong flew the Lockheed P-38 Lightning on more than 200 missions during three tours of combat duty. He downed his last enemy aircraft — a Ki-43 Oscar — over San Jose, Philippine Islands on 17 December 1944. His record was 40 victories, seven probables and 11 damaged, and he might have bettered that if he had not been "ordered" home. On his return, Bong began test flying the Lockheed P-80 jet fighter and was killed in a take-off accident at Burbank, California on 6 August 1945, just short of his 25th birthday. He had been awarded the Medal of Honor, Distinguished Service Cross, Silver star and every flying decoration with multiple oak leaf clusters. (USAF)

ACRONYMS

AA	Anti-aircraft fire
AAF	U.S. Army Air Force
A/D	Airdrome
AC	Aircraft Commander
AF	Air Force, as in 5th AF
ASV	Air Search Vessel radar
AVG	American Volunteer Group, Chinese Air Force
BB	Battleship
CAG	Carrier Air Group, also the nickname for the air group Commander
CAP	Combat air patrol
CBI	China-Burma-India theatre of combat operations
CINCPAC	Commander-in-Chief, Pacific
CO	Commanding Officer
CVE	U.S. Navy term for small escort carriers
CVL	U.S. Navy term for light aircraft carriers
CV	U.S. Navy term for large aircraft carriers
DD	Destroyer
DE	Destroyer Escort
KIA	Killed in action
LSO	Landing signal officer on an aircraft carrier
NF	Night Fighter
NMF	Natural Metal Finish
N.G.	New Guinea
PSP	Pierced Steel Planking
RAAF	Royal Australian Air Force
RAF	Royal Air Force (Great Britain)
RNZAF	Royal New Zealand Air Force
RO	Radar Operator
SN	Serial number
SWP	South West Pacific theatre of combat operations
USN	United States Navy
VB	U.S. Navy designator for a bomber or dive-bomber squadron
VC	U.S. Navy designator for a composite squadron
VD	U.S. Navy designator for a photo reconnaissance squadron
VF	U.S. Navy designator for a fighter squadron
VMB	U.S. Marine Bomber Squadron
VMF	U.S. Marine Fighter Squadron
VPB	U.S. Navy designator for a patrol bombing squadron
VP	U.S. Navy designator for a patrol squadron
VS	U.S. Navy designator for a scouting squadron
VT	U.S. Navy designator for a torpedo bombing squadron

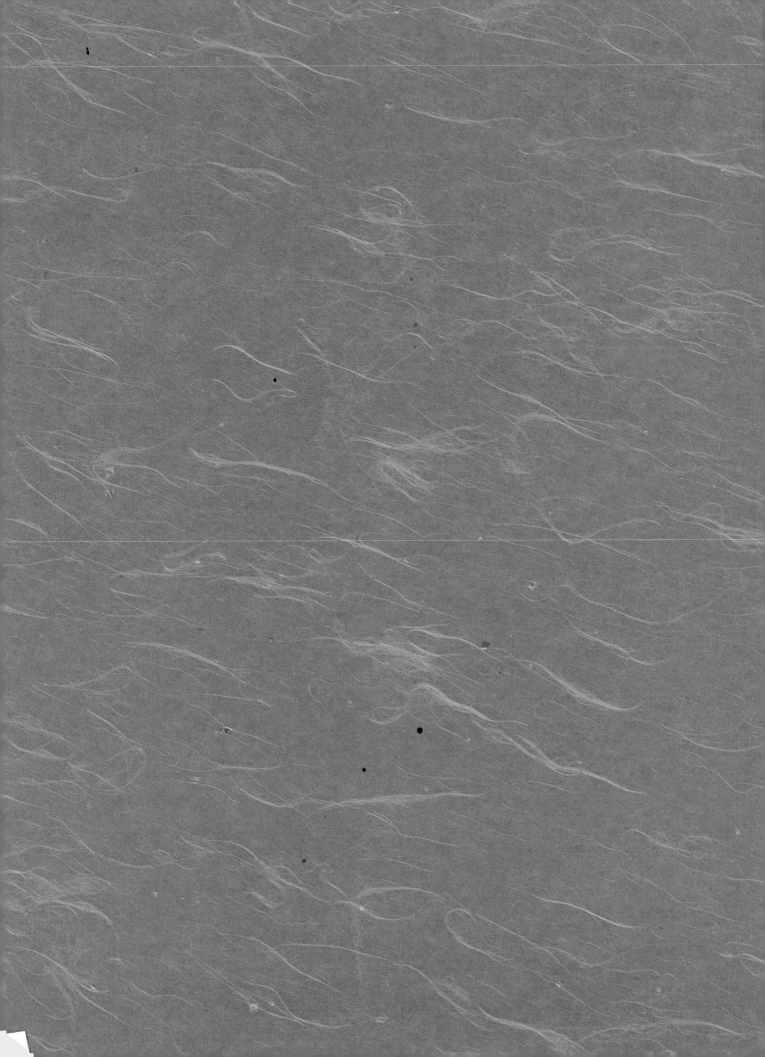